ENTIRE IDEAS

ENTIRE IDEAS

Table Of Contents

Foreword

What does creativity mean to you? To most people, they refer to the arts - writing and music for example. All the same creativity applies to everything - anything fresh, anything that's never been made before, stems from the originative mental faculty. Get all the info you need here.

Complete Concepts
Easy Solutions To Boost Your Creativity

Chapter 1:

Getting Started With Creativity

Synopsis

What are your goals, your jobs, and your spare-time activities? Can you determine how creation plays a role in that? Do you recognize that there are 2 different sorts of imagination that play a role in creativity?

The Basics

Originative Imagination

Originative imagination, which lies on the far side of our logical brain and our ego, is where all genuinely fresh ideas come from. If a scientist devises something the globe has never seen before, he's utilizing originative imagination. Consider it as fresh clay.

Edison, Bell, and Gates were brilliant inventors who learned to tap into originative imagination. Mr. Edison, for example, was reported as having tested more than 10000 ideas for his electric-light bulb utilizing his synthetic imagination alone, and they all failed. It was only if he tapped into his originative imagination that he pulled off the perfect bulb.

Synthetic Imagination

What is this synthetic imagination? This is the imagination birthed of education and experience. You apply your brain to alter things around, view them from a different angle, or rearrange existing stuff to form something "fresh". But nothing truly new ever came from synthetic imagination.

How much of what you achieve has never been witnessed before (by you, anyway)? If you author a new book, are you reorganizing stories or legends you've seen before, replacing characters, hacking and exchanging? If you write a fresh musical composition, are you really only changing one of your pet childhood songs? If you do a new marketing campaign, are you merely placing your own spin on a successful campaign already utilized by some other company?

Many modern originative thinking books available are in reality concentrating on your synthetic imagination. But there's nothing wrong with this; as a matter of fact it's a vital step. An original idea frequently needs to be fashioned by education, reasoning, and experience in order to mold a finished product.

Take the design of the cover of this book, for instance (hopefully you're reading a legal copy that has the cover). It began out as an original thought in my head, as the fresh clay of creation. I began to apply my synthetic imagination to fashion the clay.

As I began to transfer the idea out of my mind into my computer, I utilized my graphic skills to cut it down to what is conceivable with current technology. I forged the vague idea by adding together colors according to existent color scheme. I affected text and pictures into particular positions based on what I know of human computer interaction. It's only then it turns into a completed product.

Let me sidetrack a bit here. All thoughts, all goals, everything we would like to accomplish begins as an idea in our mental realms, and is forged by worldly hands. Anything human beings ever created began as a thought. Anything humankind ever produced was forged by worldly hands.

Chapter 2:

What Works For Getting The Juices Flowing

Synopsis

Brainstorming is a popular tool that helps you generate creative solutions to a topic.

It's particularly useful if you wish to break out of old, established forms of thinking, so that you are able to evolve fresh ways of viewing things. It likewise helps you defeat a lot of the issues that may make group problem-solving an uninspired and unsatisfactory process.

Some Techniques

If confronted with a challenge, resolutions might seem hard to come by. Let yourself see that this isn't really the case by writing your issue at the top of a sheet of paper and then coming up with 30 ways to solve it. These are just fast, bite-sized thoughts, not totally developed plans.

Certainly, 30 is a large number, however what you'll discover is that once you've covered the obvious stuff, your brain will begin coming up with additional and more originative approaches. Some of them will be unrealistic, however don't censor yourself till your list is done, and then you're able to go back and assess every item.

While group brainstorming is frequently better at generating thoughts than normal group problem-solving, study after study has demonstrated that if people brainstorm on their own, they come up with more thoughts (and frequently better quality thoughts) than groups of people who brainstorm together.

Partly this occurs because, in groups, people aren't always strict in following the rules of brainstorming, and bad group behaviors sneak in. Mostly, though, this occurs because people are paying so much attention to others thoughts that they're not generating thoughts of their own - or they're forgetting these thoughts while they wait for their turn to speak. This is called "blocking".

If you brainstorm on your own, you'll tend to produce a broader range of thoughts than with group brainstorming - you don't have to fret about others egos or notions, and may therefore be more freely creative. For example, you may find that an idea you'd be hesitant to bring up in a group session evolves into something quite special if you research it with individual brainstorming. Nor do you have to wait for others to quit talking before you lend your own thoughts.

You might not, however, develop thoughts as fully if you brainstorm on your own, as you don't have the broader experience of other members of a group to help you.

Alter your approach. If you're sitting in front of the PC attempting to write the next Great American Novel however plainly can't seem to get a handle on the words, you may find that you're pressing too hard in one direction. Look to other forms of expression to prompt yourself.

Attempting to author a song? Instead of listening to music, head out to the local art museum for a little visual input. Having trouble with image design? Go to the symphony and let yourself be inspired by a totally different art form.

Occasionally the key to motivation lies in the surroundings you're in. You may dread changing the tire on your car, as your garage is wet, cold and ill lit. Ask an acquaintance for the use of his well-lit, heated garage, and the job might become more pleasurable. You're able to also make the project more enjoyable by asking other people to get involved. If you ask someone to share their expertise it may be an ego boost for them and a source of support for you.

One way to ensure personal success and continued exuberance for your own path is discovering people who are successful in the matters that are meaning to you. Get to know these people, learn their attitudes and behaviors. By finding a model for success you'll have someone to emulate.

You might also look at individuals you don't wish to become and study these negative habits. Both will help you learn crucial lessons about your future; however be sure to center on the positive individual the most. It's interesting to make a list of your friends and families while examining which qualities each of these people have and the habits that make these characteristics possible.

Your model for success might not lie in the actions of one-man, however in the positive traits of all the people you interact with.

Chapter 3:

Coming Up With Fresh Ideas

Synopsis

Often, we make the mistake of presuming that advantageous ideas simply happen. Or more hazardous still, we get stuck in the mind trap that creativity is an aptitude; some people have it, others don't. Then there's the additional self-defeating belief - "I'm not bright enough to come up with advantageous ideas."

New Things

These hypotheses are seldom honest. Everyone can summon fresh, radical ideas - you simply need to discover how to open your brain and think otherwise.

Standard idea-generation techniques center on blending or adjusting existing ideas. This may surely yield results. However here, our focus is on outfitting you with tools that help you jump onto an entirely different plane. These approaches force your brain to devise fresh connections, think otherwise and consider new views.

A caution - while these techniques are highly effective, they'll only succeed if they're backed by robust knowledge of the area you're working on. This means that if you're not organized with enough data about the topic, you're unlikely to summon a dandy idea even by utilizing the techniques listed here.

By the way, these techniques may be utilized to spark creativity in group settings and brainstorming sessions likewise.

All of us tend to get attached to particular thinking patterns. Breaking these thought rules may help you get your brain unstuck and yield fresh ideas. There are many strategies you're able to use to break constituted thought patterns:

Dispute conjectures: For each state of affairs, you have a set of key conjectures. Disputing these conjectures gives you a whole fresh spin on theories.

You would like to buy something but can't since you assume you don't have the income to. Dispute the conjecture. Sure, you don't have money in the bank but couldn't you sell some of your other assets to raise the revenue? Can you dip into your retirement pension? May you work overtime and grow the pot in 6 months? Suddenly the picture begins looking brighter.

Reword the problem: expressing the problem otherwise frequently leads to a different idea. To rephrase the problem view the issue from different angles.

"Why do we need to settle the problem?", "What's the roadblock here?", "What will come about if we don't settle the issue?" These questions will give you new insights.

You might muster up new ideas to resolve your new problem.

In the fifties, shipping companies were losing on freighters. They decided they needed to concentrate on building faster and more effective ships.

However, the problem persevered. Then one advisor defined the problem otherwise. He said the issue the industry should think about was "how may we bring down cost?" The fresh issue statement yielded new ideas. All facets of shipping, including warehousing of cargo and loading time, were viewed. The result of this shift in focus ensued in the container vessel and the roll-on/roll-off freighter.

Imagine in reverse: If you feel you can't think about anything fresh, try turning things inverted. Instead of centering on how you might resolve an issue/improve operations/heighten a product, consider how could you produce the issue/worsen operations/downgrade the merchandise. The reverse thoughts will come flowing in.

Consider these ideas - once you've inverted them again - as possible solutions for the original dispute.

Show yourself another medium: We have multiple intelligences but for some reason, when faced with challenges we simply tend to utilize our verbal thinking. How about expressing the challenge through another medium? Clay, music, word affiliation games, paint, there are many ways you may convey the challenge. Don't fret about solving the challenge at this time. Just express it. A different expression might activate different thought formulas. And these fresh thought formulas might generate new ideas.

Chapter 4:

Use The Net

Synopsis

There are so many gizmos and contraptions available nowadays... you may spark your creativity online.

The Internet Can Spur Your Imagination

Utilize an online idea generator. You may get funny and inspirational ideas for anything from advice to tech support excuses.

There are billions of ways to yield ideas and come up with new concepts for your projects. You're able to utilize your subconscious to come up with an idea or you're able to consult the Idea Generator (an online tool) for random affiliations. This tool is exceptional because it gives you combinations of terms that are commonly unrelated, but your mind will still try and affiliate them. This exercise will produce lines of thoughts that may be entirely refreshing.

Add to the 3 generated words a few keywords from your own project and you get an infinite list of inspirational sentences. Most of them will be non-sense, but they could still give you a seed for an idea. Naturally you're able to simply utilize a dictionary for this purpose, but this tool is handier.

Stumped for a theme?

Invite suggestions. Do you Twitter? Facebook? Blog? Use a phone? All of these are capital ways to reach out to other originative people in order to tap into some keen ideas.

Internet social networking etiquette depends on the same principles from real life "treat others as you wish them to treat you". These etiquettes facilitate effective interaction so that social networks are not turned into a warfare zone. As, no written rules regulate 'netiquette', as web social networking is known; it broadly depends upon the sensibilities of the person.

With the spread of social networking, netiquette becomes all the more essential because it's truly easy to damage someone's reputation. Another element is that, once on the net it can't be taken back. And the data may be recalled by anyone with access to technology.

Likewise individuals form an opinion about you based on the interactions on the social network. There's always the risk of embarrassing oneself and others. It's truly hard to convey civility in internet social networking so; individuals shouldn't get offended for getting rejected or not getting any messages from a particular person.

Here is some etiquette involved in web social networking.

✓ Don't lose your head on reading negative comments and snap off an awful post. Once the send button is clicked, there's no way to recall from the web. Later you could understand your nasty comment was groundless, but you may do nothing about it.

✓ Be careful when adding friends. You're able to safely add the ones, you know. For the rest, add those whose profile matters to you.

✓ Don't paste pics of others, without their permission. Even your pics should be decent. Remember that social networking sites are your Net presence, so build your report.

✓ Don't post links of adult sites or any other illegal web sites. Likewise don't upload videos and pics which are lewd.

✓ Always give the complete and right profile. Profiles inform others of you and so don't misdirect them. Supply common background data along with your likes and dislikes.

✓ Don't spread evil rumor.

✓ Smearing other people on social networking sites is likewise bad manners. Everyone you're connected to may read what you post, so stay away from writing atrocious remarks about others.

✓ Don't junk e-mail. People get irritated when they receive spam. Spamming is likewise in bad taste.

✓ Don't keep on asking people to add you as a friend.

✓ To be efficient, update often and participate. Post daily and comment on others posts.

✓ Smiles may be utilized to denote a tone. However, use it meagerly. Similarly, don't use all capitals in your message posts. Utilizing all capitals is the online version of screaming.

✓ If someone posts you a comment, reply.

✓ The less abbreviation you practice the better it is. Utilize only those abbreviations that are reasonably common, as you will not be there to explain.

✓ Be as brief as possible and to the point. People neither do have the time nor the patience to read page long ramblings.

✓ In case of any arguments, focus on the issues rather than the individuals involved.

✓ Keep an open mind. Don't get mucked up in message wars...

Chapter 5:

It Doesn't Have To Be Either Or

Synopsis

We might achieve Project A or Project B. Do you want more time or more earnings? You're able to have a great life and average career or fair life and exceptional career. I've got yellow or red, which do you want?

Win or lose. Yes or no. The world is black or white. You're able to have this or that. Which do you select? We have to choose.

All of the statements and questions above are cases of either/or thinking. All of them pre-suppose that we live in a world bounded by the choice of either this or that - one or the other.

These statements are based on the belief that our world is confined. All of these choices are basically rooted in the "lack mentality."

I believe there's an another choice. This choice will give you more options; it will better your outlook and attitude and the caliber of your life. (It similarly might lend greatly to bettering your standard of living).

Changing It

The following are some tips to follow in the quest to overhaul the property and yet bust the bank:

This 2nd approach amplifies our thinking and is founded on a notion that there's plenty in the world for everyone - plenty of time, chances, revenue, resources, people, fun, and experiences. I call it both/and" thinking. This mindset is rooted in the "abundance mentality."

We began with either/or options. Let's concentrate on just one (you're able to apply the logic and approach on any of the others - or anything else in your life) and regard two project opportunities with a both/and mentality. Start by asking . . . "How can we achieve both Projects A and B?"

By asking the question you're scrapping the underpinning of the lack mentality; by asking the question you're opening yourself to fresh theories.

Don't have enough people to do both projects? If both have a favorable reward, why not get a little supplemental help either on the projects or on other work to free up time for the projects?

The aim of both/and thinking is to open us up to more options and opportunities.

Don't have enough money to act on both projects? What if you establish a partner? Who else might benefit?

At this point, you may be thinking that if we keep saying "yes" we'll never have any focus or achieve superior results in the options we make. Of course we still have to prioritize and make selections. The concept of both/and thinking is to open us up to more options and chances before directly moving to instituting a choice between A or B.

If you trust that the world is filled with a lot of possibilities and that there are always more options to consider, then you'll feel completely comfortable asking these sorts of queries. If we live in an either/or world, we're directly settling for one or the other before we even consider that something more or different is imaginable.

There are some keys to acquiring and utilizing "both/and" thinking. Realize that initially (and finally) employing this mental approach is a habit - a habit that you're able to sustain and grow.

Believe in abundance. It begins with a notion that more is available to us - in terms of hypotheses, resources, chances and approaches. Once we trust this is true we'll begin our search for more options.

Run on faith. Even if your belief of abundance isn't yet firm, run on faith. Have faith that it's true, even if you can't see it or feel it yet.

Question. To see the options you have to question, "why not both?" Or versions like, "How can we do both?" "What would we have to alter or adjust to attain both of these?" "Why do we have to pick?" You get the idea.

Consider the theories. When you've asked the question, be hospitable to the options and you'll be amazed at how many will turn up for you.

What you're able to achieve now.   You're coping with some situation right now. How are you thinking of it? Are you thinking either/or or both/and? If you're thinking of either/or take the steps above - try both/and thinking. Attempting it is the opening move - and that's a step you're able to take immediately.

Chapter 6:

Synopsis

There's a true reality to taking a break.

This is something I got from all my books on how to be originative (the things I do for you, my dear readers!). Often after a break, I find errors, poor flow, or fresh views that I couldn't see due to familiarity sightlessness. Walk away from brainstorming session and go back in a few hours or a couple of days. You'll be surprised at what you get popping up your brain.

Take A Pause

- 27 -

Do you from time to time get ground to a halt when authoring material, analyzing, designing, or engaged in another creative enterprise? Or maybe you simply can't get rolling; you go through writer's block or blank out. The void page or screen may be daunting.

And so, take a break! I've determined that transferring from one sort of activity to a different one arouses creativity. This is especially true when transitioning from work to leisure time, exercise, or a hobby. Perhaps by resting our conscious mind we put into action our subconscious.

Consider a recent illustration. One break of the day, first thing, I began working on a proposal to print a third edition of one of my books. After approximately 2 hours, I had a good start, including an outline and a little bit of text.

Even so, I started to get stuck and as well get hungry. I biked to a nearby restaurant and, while savoring a light breakfast, 3 proposal-related thoughts "bulged" into my head. I wrote of them on the backside of paper placemats.

I then began a ten-mile bicycle ride, during which I stopped 3 times to briefly jot down more thoughts that came along "out of the blue."

More of late, I followed exactly the same formula - breakfast and a 10 mile bicycle ride - and, on the ride and out of nowhere, I determined how to structure a report that was in the really early stages.

These certain situations are typical of many standardized originative experiences I've enjoyed over the years that were aroused by "shifting gears." Taking a break betters personal effectiveness and efficiency.

Wrapping Up

You're so originative.

Don't deny it. Whether or not you think about yourself a creative sort, the truth is that you're perpetually producing ideas.

Mindfulness and these strategies invite you to be aware of this perpetually flowing river, and provides an opportunity to choose to sit beside it instead of swimming in it. By watching the ideas from that calm riverside (your inner being), you are able to more clearly see the ones that float to the top and glisten in the sun.

But mindfulness is more than just mind watching mind... It's the strategies here. When we're engaged in the process of creating-- whether that's words, numbers, music, art, or movement--without getting swept up in the concept of where it may be leading, that's a very pure form of mindfulness.